TODAY WAS MY FIRST VIOLIN LESSON

WRITTEN AND ILLUSTRATED BY RAFAEL RAMIREZ

DIGITALIZED BY NORMAN BERMUDEZ

EDITED BY MARIA A. BERMUDEZ

©2014 Rafael Ramirez.

Hi, my name is Gabriel.

Today was my first violin lesson.

My Mom told me that I will learn how to play violin.

We went to my teacher's Violin Studio.

Mr. Ramirez is my violin teacher.

My teacher told me about

the different parts of the violin...

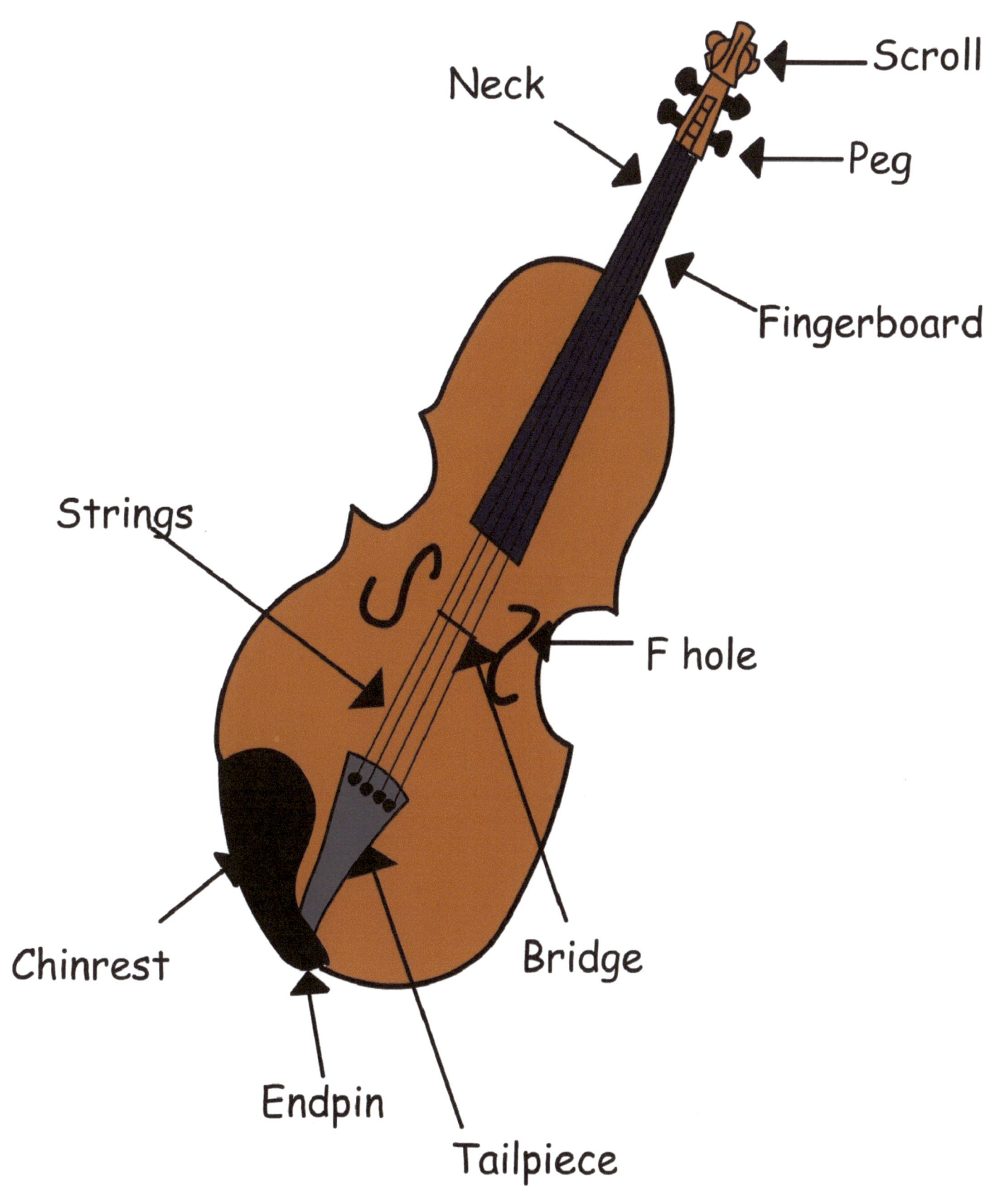

...And

the parts of the bow.

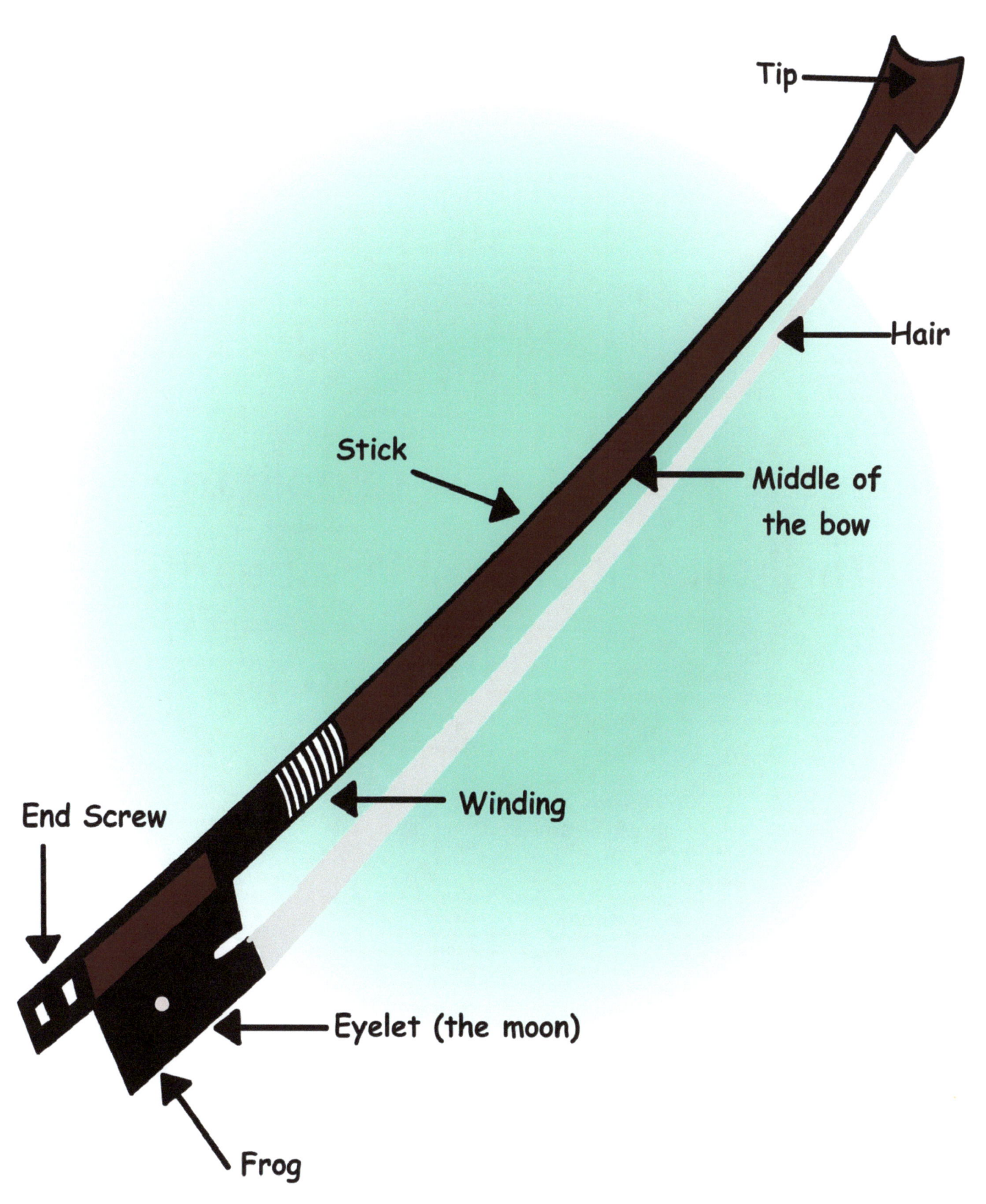

I need to practice how to hold the bow. This will help me make a beautiful sound.

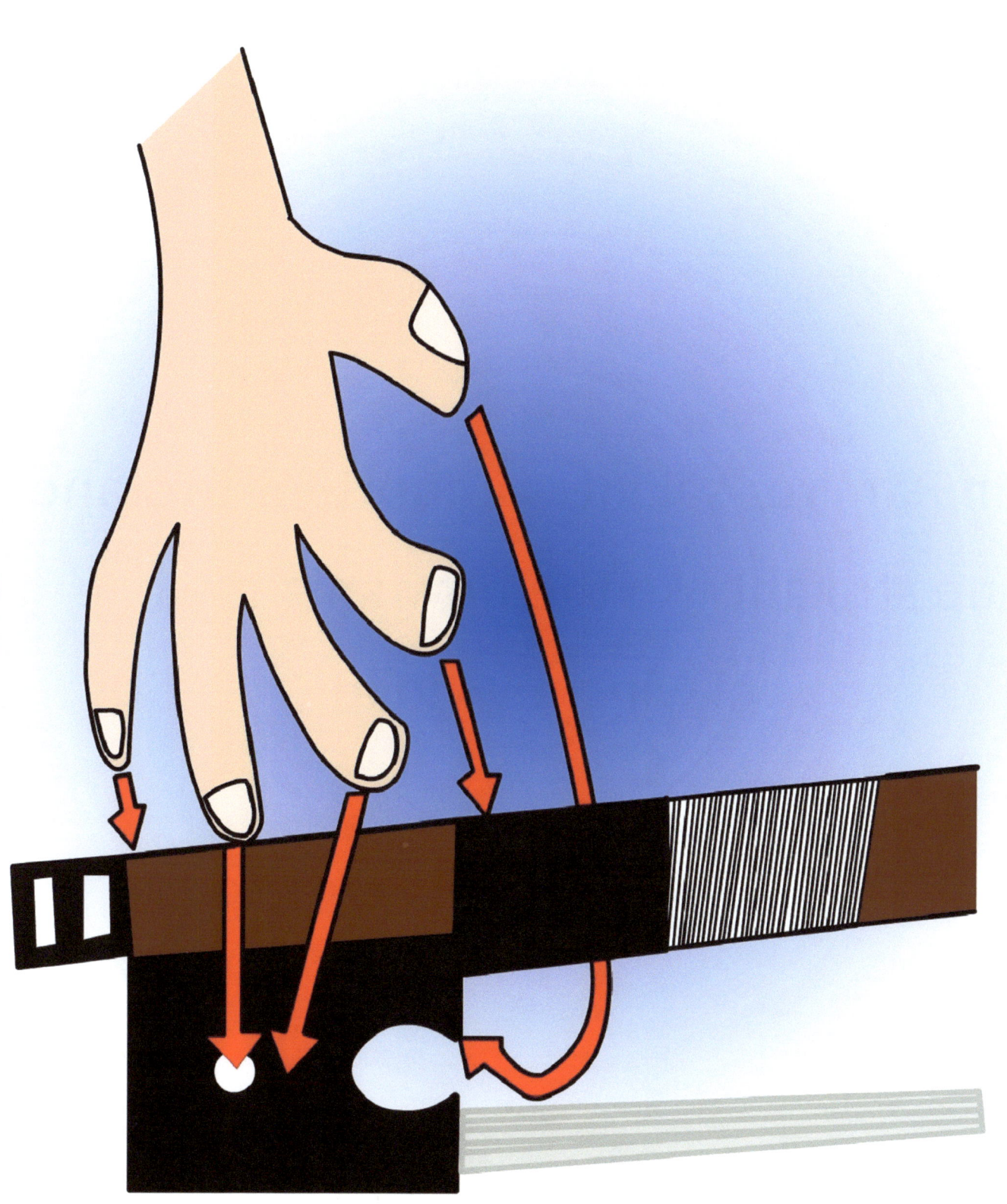

Mr. Ramirez said it is important to stand up straight like the bow knight while playing my violin.

I learned how to do down bow(Π)...

...and up bow (V).

Mr. Ramirez said:

"The bow has to go stright like a train to make a beautiful sound."

I learned about:

The music staff. It is used to notate music.

The pitches – The musical notes, and the type of notes.

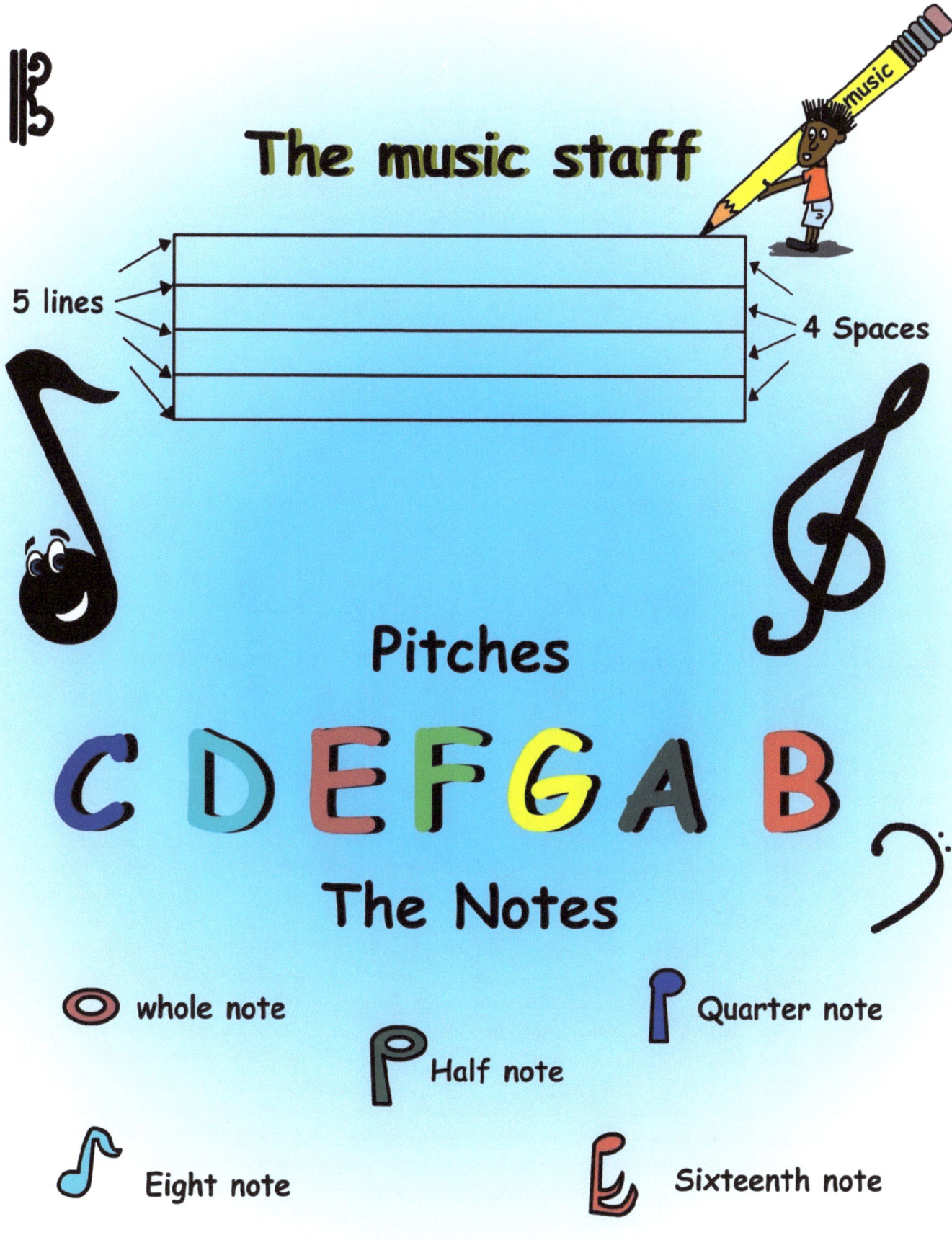

I love to play my violin.

My teacher surprised me at the end of the lesson with a piece of candy and my first violin book.

I love to have violin lessons.

www.ingramcontent.com/pod-product-compliance
Lightning Source LLC
Chambersburg PA
CBHW041231040426
42444CB00002B/123